FAIRY ROCK

ALSO BY STEPHEN WATT

Spit (Bonacia Ltd, 2012)
Optograms (Wild Word Press, 2016)
MCSTAPE (Last Night From Glasgow, 2018)

FAIRY ROCK

A Crime Novel in Verse

STEPHEN WATT

Annie,

Absolutely love your music + our wee gig together in Monifieth!

Enjoy the book & catch you 3/11 at Oran Mor!

RED SQUIRREL PRESS

First published in 2019 by Red Squirrel Press
36 Elphinstone Crescent
Biggar
South Lanarkshire
ML12 6GU
www.redsquirrelpress.com

Typesetting and design by Gerry Cambridge
e: gerry.cambridge@btinternet.com

Text Copyright © Stephen Watt 2019
The right of Stephen Watt to be identified as the author of this work has been asserted by him in accordance with Section 77 of the Copyright, Designs and Patents Act 1988. All rights reserved.

Cover images: Skull: Pattang/Shutterstock;
Silhoutte of Ailsa Craig: Ales Micola/Shutterstock;
Curling Stone: FOS_ICON/Shutterstock.

A CIP catalogue record is available from the British Library.

ISBN: 978 1 910437 84 1

Red Squirrel Press is committed to a sustainable future. This book is printed in the UK by Imprint Digital using Forest Stewardship Council certified paper.
www.digitalimprint.co.uk

*This book is dedicated to my darling sister, Susan,
whose love for crime novels and loaning of
Stuart MacBride books was the beginning of all this.*

CONTENTS

Degloving | 11
Twos | 12
Paddy's Market | 13
Bugs | 14
Candles | 15
Orphanage | 16
Order | 17
Vivisection | 18
Meringue | 19
Fight | 20
Zante | 21
Chib | 22
Calton Roulette | 24
Glasgow Soldier | 25
Theatre | 26
Own Medicine | 27
Tip-off | 28
Drinking Den | 29
Courier | 31
Tongland | 33
Walk | 34
Monsters | 35
Marble | 36
Homesick | 37
Cyberstalking | 38
Dynamation | 39
Hunt | 40
Pixels | 41
Old Firm Day | 42
Inheritance | 43
Walk On | 44
Banked | 45

Whose Funeral? | 46
Dead Meat | 47
Gloaming | 48
Court | 49
Lost Ark | 50
Rendezvous | 51
Bail | 52
Preacher | 53
Setbacks | 54
Shipment | 55
Pathway | 56
Crucifixion | 57
Recce | 58
Peak | 59
Bargaining | 60
Curling | 61
Security | 62
Straw Man | 63
Tabloid Haiku | 64
Analysis | 65
Shredded | 66
Grave | 67
Whale Tapes | 68
Safe House | 69
Clubbing | 70
Lightning Strikes | 71
Chips Protocol | 72
Requiem | 73
Molly | 74
Modus Operandi | 75
Standoff | 76
Florist | 77
Toxicology | 78
Bloodsucking | 79

Girvan | 81
Omnipresent | 82
Convoy | 83
Zoom | 84
Names | 85
End Credits | 86
Sentence | 87
Miracles | 88
Fairy-tale | 89

Acknowledgments | 91

A NOTE ON THE TYPE | 92

DEGLOVING

1977 –

In some sort of bloodied, fang-clamp,
the short woman kept a holdfast jaw-vice
on the bouncer's organ outside The White Elephant,
vehemently wrenching her head
and spitting bits of scrotum
from out of the corners of her mouth.

Onlooking diners in the Chinese restaurant
beneath the nightclub
retched into oriental table lamps, gagging
at Sauchiehall Street's latest revolting scene
while the bouncer's screams ricocheted the length of the street.

Then silence. Nauseating, traumatic stillness.
He had soiled himself. Six foot four
of stained, timbered, brown-red denim
lay twitching on the pavement, dribbling
like Tennent's into Glasgow's drains.

Distant sirens closed in
as Petra Balders wiped her crimson mouth
with one Disco Doll rabbit fur coat sleeve
and struck a match to light a cigarette,
savouring the frenzied unrest
which only the unhinged can conjure.

TWOS

In the playpark dark,
the red glow switches fingers and mouths,
blows halos above hoods – angels barren of faces,
breathing in the stars
from their perch at the top of the chute.

It is passed to Deek. Pincer claws grip the roach, singes
a thumbnail, and sucking for too long, inhales
     heaven into lung.
     He can taste them all.

Savouring the tang of Jennie's bubble-gum lips,
his tongue backflips, rolls smog and spice,
oscillates like a tantric sex swing
he once read Sting apparently indulges in
and exhales lung into heaven.

This time, there is no cough.
He hogs the joint, grins wildly
at the innocents, then trades
for cider nicked from the off-license,

hoping for Jennie's taste once more on the rim.

PADDY'S MARKET

Cardboard boxes burst open under the weight of bric-a-brac.

Cilla Black vinyl at second-hand stalls
would often conceal counterfeit tobacco
behind Winnie Boyle's endless rails
and illicit alcohol was traded inside deceptive aerosols
to ladies draped in counterfeit mink fur.

Seamus once remembered Paddy's Market fondly.
Where warped table legs were arranged
with enough mismatched shoes to garb a Cinderella army.
Pipe smoke wafted from flat-capped vendors,
shrouding his Dublin-born ma', urging her to *buy the wean a toy*
but knowing that there was no money
for such frivolous splurges.

The Clyde's sewer-stench absorbed the hanging washing-line
                                                           pillowcases
dangling between weedgrown tenements
where the soldier manifested like a ghost
from between the milky cotton sheets
carrying the letter he would never read

about the father he would never see again.

BUGS

It doesn't mean he'll become a serial killer
but Danny loves the way insects squirm
immediately before their deaths.

Pinning down one end, he can scissor
a worm in two using just his fingers.
One time in school, he caressed a feathery moth
until its crispy wings crumbled, splintered
like salt into his jotter
before tipping its spirit like smoky dandruff
into Claire Ferguson's curls.
Home, he was King. Ravaged cobwebs,
Danny plucked arachnids from harp strings
and severed their legs until all that was left
was an hourglass drained of time

        and the bluebottles dotted along the windowsills
        become an ellipsis of what is still to come.

CANDLES

Hunched, crouching, our hooded skeletons
light a candle-spoon to Jesus. Offer a prayer in case he listens.

Me, I love him. He means well. Only steals
so that we may eat. Only beats me until I can feel.
His blood is inside of me, and I him. Puts the ring into syringe.

I know the value of a woman's skin.
The way men worship them, control them, medicine
for their aching loins. My daddy showed me that.

He exemplified how some boys
like to demonstrate how strong they can be.
Nothing tougher than a former soldier
sodomising his own daughter.
Be the best. Mum's the word never spoken.

No witnesses. Ducks in the canal yell obscenities at us
but my man disposes of them with bricks.
I'm not much of an animal lover, but still –

sleep is as important to us as the housing waiting list.

Tomorrow, I turn fifteen. World at my feet,
in a rucksack. Dream big as a pipe sucking in the moon,
and relax. Light the candles, the spoon.
Sweet Jesus.

ORPHANAGE

The Catholic Sisters' up-turned, white cornettes
reminded Seamus of Devil horns.

Unable to survive with his father gone,
his mother had converted to spirits
and placed the eight-year old into care,
promising to visit the Lanark orphanage.

Bed-wetting was punished with cold baths,
spankings, being locked in dark rooms or starved.
Seamus envisaged his rib cage had a draught
that mice could dash up and down,
building their nests in the empty peel of his heart.

Other kids suffered too.
Force-fed to eat grass, caned with clubs,
the abuse was covered up by medics
who washed their hands when they took off their gloves
and when it rained a deluge, Seamus
would take refuge in the small hut
which the gardener, James, occupied.

Balming his lips with ash-black fingers,
James would slip Seamus out of his saturated trousers,
leaking shoes and holey socks
then permit the thorns of his concealed thistle tattoo
to prickle all of Seamus's subsequent nightmares.

ORDER

If he wanted to juke school,
Deek would need to help his Dad
at the café. That was his Mum's rule.
Scrubbing pots with steel wool then sponging plates
which swam in bean sauce, solidified grease and mushroom funk
was enough to make Deek think twice
about bunking. The customers were equally revolting.

A number referred to his Dad as 'Brother'
although no blood relation was known.
Talking in hushed tones and coded tongues,
pressing thumbs on knuckles, small parcels were exchanged
under the PVC-coated tables.
Like hot water bottles, only – not.

On the drive home, Deek's Dad tutted
at the freshly spray-painted UVF slogan
on the side of the Forge roundabout.
Morons, he muttered before slipping out his mobile phone
to straighten out this act of vandalism
from one of his very, very many contacts
under his own corrupt influence of tribalism.

VIVISECTION

By thirteen, James was no longer interested in him.
Seamus could recline beneath the cherry blossom,
inspiring his lungs with its ruby fruit fragrance
in the crows' playground,
safe that he wouldn't be found; or violated.

A leaf on its side could look like a knife in certain lights
but he let his mind slide to a time in his life
when he had something, someone on his side.

Yesterday, one of the other orphans
with the ever-changing adoption names,
had found a dead frog near the pond.
When dared to lick its clammy back,
Seamus had read that every toad is a frog
but not every frog is a toad
and opted not to put his life in hazard.

Its bloated corpse remained unburied,
attracting the zizzing bluebottles
which would inevitably perish on the sills of James' hut.

Carefully, using a stolen pen-knife, Seamus cut the frog's skin,
de-boning and fleshing out the edible meat,
heedful to the poisoned hallucinogens
which would plainly lead to beatings
with demon-dreams thereafter.

He had become quite the survivalist.
Now he just needed a cause to put it into practise.
A purpose for his talent.

MERINGUE

House parties were becoming harsher.
Faces looked as ruptured as the painted eggshells
found at the bottom of the Campsie hills during Easter,
and Deek wanted *in*.

In the kitchen, two fair-haired lads conversed,
polishing beaks and harvesting gums
with dust on their tongues

and chopping block knives flared
from their reddened, sore eyes when Deek loomed near.
One razor-slit grin beckoned him in.

Rolling the Queen's portrait, a dust-stripe was presented
and snorted emphatically without question.

Something wasn't right.
Brassy mule laughter erupted as Fair Hair #1 exhibited a packet
from which a crushed meringue had been ingested.
Scarlet-red, Deek dissolved into awkward hysterics
while Fair Hair #2 prepared the authentic score.

A new friendship had commenced.

FIGHT

Si's insults about Danny's cut-price clothes
had triggered a brawl on the football pitch
outside old St James Primary School.
Fist collided with bone, struck skull, drew blood from lip
or nose while a crowd circled round them,
goading them on to murder –
or at very least, leave the other comatose.

Green Street must have been lit by a werewolf moon and stars
when one of Si's uncles scuttled from the Calton Bar
before stumbling on to the concrete pitch
where a drift of tubby pigs pounded their baton sticks
over the defenceless prey.

Danny licked his swollen lip as Si hared from one fight to another,
thrashing his clenched mitts against the back of the officers.
As one swung his baton back to attack
whatever was beating his hi-vis vest,
it was Danny who shouted loudest above the rampage,
camera phone in hand, recording.

The cop stopped, laughing.
Returning his stick to belt before straightening the twisted vest,
he pointed directly at Danny warning that he would be next
to receive the treatment Si's uncle had sustained.

As the sirens cooled in the distance, Si nodded over to Danny;
an alliance commenced over an abhorrence for the law.

ZANTE

Lads holiday. Zante. A diet of fry-ups, Guinness
and pills, surrounded by beautiful, tanned Latinos
around the pool, was just what the doctor ordered
(albeit, not on an NHS prescription pad).

In Cherry Bay Beach Club,
Deek can still detect the sweet skunk smell
which had caused him to fall ill, addled
by migraine-inducing LED lights
and hoaching spray of the fog machine
jumbling contents inside his stomach,
shuffling liver and kidneys like playing cards.

Other lads, excited to be the same blood type,
are guzzling paraffin, using lubricants,
snorting contaminated mixing agents
that makes their eyes spin
like dishes balanced on crooked canes.

          She rolls an inviting finger at him.
Teeth, filed like a vampire. Hot language,
as pointed as the nipples through her top,
slide his weak hand into the honeyed wetlands
of her teen spirit   until Deek retches,
watches his own reflection yodelling in a mirror
as a Jackson Pollock drip painting
heaves over the glass, between her breasts
and down the Adidas vest
he had nicked from a folded pile in Sports Direct.

CHIB

Sitting next to Daniel in Modern Studies class,
it was Laura who spotted the charcoal sketch
on the inside cover of his jotter.

A man in a black ski mask
appeared to wedge a combat knife
into some poor wretch's blood-drenched face,
saturating the olive camouflage jacket
of this particular unfortunate soldier.
She had seen these depictions before.

Men, with candelabras of knives for fingers,
spearing tridents and severing limbs
like Poseidon executing deserters who had betrayed him.
Daniel hadn't seemed so unusual in primary school
but at Holyrood Secondary he had become angry,
resentful with the army for whatever reason.

To him, the hunger strikes in the late-seventies
were as impressive as the moon landings in the late-sixties
and when he divulged the concealed blade
used to carve Laura's initials on a playground tree,
she knew how mercurial he could be.
His face pretzelled when he rubbed his thumb
over the point, pocking indentations
until excitable blood run, bandaged by tongue.
The shape in his trousers, swelling like an alarm bell.

She remembered the final time she saw him.
The cuffs restraining his wrists.
His reddened watery eyes, pupils quivering
like unanswered coins inside a wishing well

as an officer jostled his bowed, long-haired head
into the rear seat of the patrol car.
Laura's guidance teacher cooing in her ear
that she did the *right thing to report this.*

Expelled. It sounded so official.
The charcoal thumbprint on her neck,
burning like a Judas kiss.

CALTON ROULETTE

The fuse to the rocket had been lit
upon one of the kiddie's swings.
Squeals of alarm pre-empted
the spinning firework's launch,
sending teenage boys scattering
into spiralling, track-suited Catherine Wheels.

Across the drizzling, golden atoms,
Danny locked eyes with a titanic nuclear bomb,
standing steady. Fists balled like detonator boxes, ready
for the rocket's combustion.

There was mutual appreciation here.
No shitebaggery. Death or Glory.
The rocket shot quickly towards Danny,
zoomed a kiss into his left lughole
before shattering the upstairs window of a nearby brothel.
The curled, snail-shelled manhood
of one, elderly, bespectacled client
was visible to all when he caterwauled
half the names in the Bible
out the ruptured glass into the busy street below.

The two new laughing friends shook hands,
sharing a palm-sized bottle
of something red, sweeter than sugar.

Danny McAllister, big man. He winced
at his own half-hearted whisper.
The colossus replaced the moon's face
and in its place, growled back *Tommy Greeber.*

GLASGOW SOLDIER

A footslog of men subsisted in the city centre.
Motorcyclists synthesised with their bikes
and sunless, oily goths leaked out of the engines
into ticket queues outside the shops.
Pavilion staff never suspected
that the older men had smuggled drams
inside of hot water bottles
while the Celtic faithful shuffled towards the Jungle
carrying piss-cans inside of olive-khaki parka jackets.

Seamus looked on as a broad-shouldered Adonis
positioned himself at the entrance
of the army recruitment office
and twinkled at the way other men swerved
round his stockpiled shadow.

The hailstorm-slit poppy petals shimmered like a red carpet
where the soldier held the door open
wearing a smile as broad as a career;
a cigarette burning like a lit passion.

THEATRE

It had been less than two years.
Rehearsals had been gruelling, replicating
the same steps on the school stage.
Memorising her lines from dog-eared pages,
Claire revelled in the theatre elbow room
which allowed her to be someone else.

Stage spotlights withered to Wonderland pill-size.
Car headlights cruised past,
beaming their lecherous eyes
down her knee-high boots,
the bronzed, palm-size, caramel-silk of her thighs.

In the back of many she saw car seats
strapped in. Half-sucked lollies and playthings,
children's strewn imaginations
that their Daddies were good men.

Cached in an underpass, her boyfriend booked the rooms,
posted ads, counted the cash which he pledged
would be invested in a house and a car.
His Melpomene mask fixed rigidly over his sneer.

A van pulled to the kerb. Someone rolled down his window
where a guff of weed reeked and a mattress in the rear
bloomed with spunk stains and burst springs.

Showtime.

OWN MEDICINE

Like a punctured sex doll, the crumpled
pelt of his friend lolled in the armchair.
Combed, platinum hair was now reddened
as a glossy tomato flattened upon the head
and a shattered picture frame
resembled how Deek remembered him.

His puppet-marbled eye twitched inside its teabag socket
towards his own disjointed limb, snipped of string and strength
while bubbles of gurgling breath
cork-popped, saluting his own impending death.

The other man standing in the room
polished the heavy iron mallet
with the end of his waterproof jacket,
rinsing blood off in the kitchen sink.
His long, sooty chin linked him
as an associate from his Dad's café.

Stepping over the wreckage of the body,
the stranger winked, whispering *Call an ambulance now
if you wish him to live*, before vanishing into the alley
where the junkies had all dissipated.

Deek thumbed the '9' of his phone,
contemplating that time his new friends had deserted,
leaving him all alone to take the punishment
of the polis who had raided the party
and then he waited; meditated
to the gurgling petition of the armchair.

TIP-OFF

PB, AKA Petra Balders, is five foot three of witch alder –
the spiked, white flower which blossoms in Alabama.

DI Lisa Jackson knew that Balders
was responsible for the slaughter
of several drug dealers in and around the Barras markets.
The most famous one being Daryl Hotchkiss
whose bludgeoned skull was crushed into chalk-dust
with an adjacent Ailsa Craig-constructed curling stone.

Double-cross PB and it was widely known in Glasgow
that her boys would come hunting.

The police couldn't get near.
Concealed cameras were detected in the family homes.
Inside of vents and light fittings,
units in kitchens positioned on the table
where cutting agents and samples
would serve as evidence in court,
aborted by any one of the four brothers
on their daily sweep of their cupboards.

But Jackson had a tip-off from a source
that narcotics were being transported
from Edinburgh by one of PB's dealers
residing beneath the disused Polmadie Bridge.

The Surveillance Team were positioned.
The interview questions were drafted.
Research was made into the boy's family and girlfriend
while Jackson chewed on her plastic pen lid,
determined for one tactic to finally work.

DRINKING DEN

Greeber was a monster.
Six foot nine of towering hulk,
radio-faced, choler-skinned, his contour with the sun behind
eclipsed a football pitch.

The People's Palace gargled the last of the day's light
like mouthwash, spitting its red gum disease
across Glasgow Green where Greeber, Danny, Si, and Joe
were camouflaged by dense shrubs.

The devil dug was on its own,
snarling its demented word stock
like it was trained for police work.
Greeber had simply had enough.

Gripping the woolly nape of its neck,
the Alaskan heritage and upper strength
of the dog failed to grapple, wrestle its driving legs away
from Greeber embracing its convulsing frame
into his red, brick-wall chest.
They build them to last in the Calton.

The dog's savage fangs slivered strips of his shoulder
until it slowed, sedated, suffocated
in his Herculean arms. Its scarlet, lifeless tongue
sat lop-sided, a caricature of what it once was.
Greeber lay the asphyxiated dog in the grass,
finger muzzling mouth to instruct the lads to keep hush
as a man carrying a leash howled for his absent pet.

Joe and Si looked as rattled as snakes but Danny cackled,
shaking behind the shrubs

as Greeber slid his bloodied fingers and nails
down his own face like some Hindi horror scene,
dyed in Native American war-paint
and still only sixteen.

COURIER

The musty gleam of dried-in pish on the toilet floor
made Claire retch.
Instructed to remain hidden, she had bolted the door
shut before the Megabus inched its way out the city
towards the capital, professing pregnancy
to anybody who came close between her feigned dry-heaves.

Edinburgh's autumn-flagged leaves
and cannon smoked stone
emitted the burnt carcasses of vampires
in its sunlit vapours; a bank of dense fog
and hoof dust gyrating like frothing spectres
inside the old city's walls
until the tourist trap and its Nessie dolls
spewed from every shop's entrance.

Farther still, she walked beyond the cobbles'
bone-tired haunted walks, past Calton Hill
and the Meadows
until the black spiked gates of Grange Cemetery
rose like thorny shadows out of the ground.

At the statue of the angel holding a flower
and pointing towards Heaven stood her arranged visitant;
face masked by the sculpture's outline.
PB's girl? he gravelly questioned.
Claire stood still, nodding – unsure if he could see
her head moving before his ratty frame scuttled towards her.
It's all there, he murmured, extending
a weighty square pattern into her hands
before vanishing down some hidden drain.

Some other person would courier the payment, but for now
all Claire had to do was return the way she came.
Obscure her squared ribs, avoid the public,
advance through the perilous darkness
until she was back inside the bus toilets
weaving her way towards the canal
where her boyfriend would be waiting.

Nobody would ever have expected a girl.

TONGLAND

Released from Polmont one month premature
for good behaviour,
Deek placed his rucksack next to the hallway furniture
and found his Dad standing by the cooker,
demolishing beans out of a rusting pot.

It had never occurred to him. *Before*.
Affiliations dictated by Calton streets
when young boys existed on chains and razors,
carving meat off the shoulders and fingers.
It was never just blood on concrete
but planted flags of a man's intention.
A declaration of one's masculinity tested in Mugger's Alley
where the life expectancy of the Calton
squared off at the ripe age of fifty-three.

Deek knew now that his father was more Mason than Tong.
Less rook, more pawn
but like any strategic General from the bygone Tongland,
cross him at your peril.
He had survived this long, with good reason.

WALK

Swapping drugs for drums came naturally to Deek.
Faither, uncles, cousins in and around Bridgeton
enlisted him for the cause, purring about Belfast
and Catholic corruption.
Nothing would please King William more
than singing about the Boyne, banging drums and storming lungs
into flutes in the neighbourhoods *they* lived in.

Mould, on decayed living-room walls,
coupled with tar rotting his teeth,
swayed the instrument of choice for Deek.
At Bridgeton Cross, the band practised for July's marches,
spinning batons and spitting venom while he beat curved canes
against the goat skin of his Lambeg drum –
muscles and veins protruding like blue, silky sashes on his scruff.

Late-June, outside the Sacred Heart,
a funeral procession inched on through Bridgeton
behind a white, arm's-length coffin
dwarfed inside a crawling hearse.
A grunt expressed between Deek's nasal passage
and the motorcycle-blood of his puss hoicks black mucus
on to the front glass of one mourner's car

where inside, Danny imprints Deek's face to mind, redirecting
all the pain of his baby sister's cot death
into mutilating this fat bastard; make walking a fond fairy-tale
from a distant, Dutch courage past.

MONSTERS

In the Necropolis, the sparking lighter wheel
flared the horror monsters moving upon its stones –
the raven, Hyde, Count Orlok and Glasgow Cathedral's bats
whose jittery wings stirred the poisoned dark
into frantic, dancing mosaics.

Near the Bridge of Sighs,
Claire's eyes struggled in the crepuscular gloom.
Her own condensation suspired souls to ascend out the ground
and divine vampires with iron teeth
to cache behind the bark of crooked trees
then swill from their full, lifeblood syringes.

A temper of nightingales
hurtled, haunted through her veins,
squalling when her father's taunting face
projected on to the cemetery gates –
eating the restless consciousness,
slipping sleep down like a pair of pants to the ankles.

MARBLE

Since losing his wife Gina to cancer eight months ago,
Frank has devoted himself to the House of God.
Removing the awkward plastic numbers
from the buckled, oak hymn board,
Father Redmond offers good-natured thanks
for Frank's amateur turn on the organ
despite his jaded, jarring warbling
muddling the rest of the congregation.

Scrounging a tealight, Frank poaches a pre-lit prayer
to the side of the altar and allows the licking flame
to melt wax-threads from the stone-mosaic of his goffered eyes.
His own heels echo emphatically on the cool, white marble
like an archangel standing behind;
the spirit of his love dances in the colours
of the stained-glass windows at the rear of the church.

Coins in the baskets clink like fruit machines
into the hessian pouch used to carry the collections to the bank.
As Frank fumbles for keys in the deep pockets
of his unseasonal winter coat, the marbled footsteps
return – doubled – and bring the heavy metallic
cross of the Lord down upon his head.

Stunned by Satan, he shifts into the black magic
of sleep, the tinkle of hoisted change – his lullaby,
and distorted shouting petitioning
Claire to *leave him and fucking run*.

The marble is as cool as Gina's kiss upon his cheek.

HOMESICK

Seaweed perfumes breakfast oats on cyan-stringed waves
which whisk contaminated dolphin milk
with inanimate marine life bobbing beneath their boat.
Seamus had adored every minute of seeing the world
with the only family he'd ever known
but currents were towing him home.

He had seen enough death; lost a hand and crushed bones
on behalf of a country
he felt he still didn't know – or appreciate.

One more month and then it was time to address life.

CYBERSTALKING

It was so easy. A false profile created online
using some dead Austrian hooligan's picture,
the isolation of Danny's dingy bedsit
was mobile-lit on his kisser when he found him.
Swathed in a 'No Surrender' flag
among the loyalist mecca of one Orange Order,
Derek 'Deek' Ronaldson was tagged on social media;
a Calton-native not seven streets away.
Friend requested, added, and embryonic
chat initiated – and Danny was in.

Casework and guesswork led to other social networks
where family followers freely scattered snippets of knowledge –
favourite drummers, cars, lovers and most importantly
Deek's Rangers season ticket seat number.

The Old Firm match at Ibrox was in a few weeks.
Tickets, of course, wouldn't be easy to come by
but this would be inconsequential
if he was successful tomorrow
at the Safety Steward's job interview.

Suddenly, Danny was mindful
that his NVQ Level 2 qualification may finally prove useful.

DYNAMATION

Paying tribute to the savage giant cyclopes
in Homer's 'Odyssey', army friends had informally
named him *Phemus* after an explosive mine
accidentally discharged on a military training exercise.
One scorched doll's eye shunted towards his nasal bridge
and like a Harryhausen creation,
he twitched, shifted damaged bones frame by frame
like a stop-motion picture being filmed in the Gallowgate.

Past the vinegary taxi ranks and weed-perfumed council vans,
Phemus' bald, ugly structure lumbered between shady Irish bars
which cops relished to monitor.
Rumour whispered like Tolbooth traitors
that he had partaken in Satanic rituals
and that unfortunate homeless individuals
had meat sucked from their bones like crabs
inside their stopgap squats;
their metacarpals suited for dental floss.

Such nightmarish skinder hindered an ability to ever get close.
Abusing any bar's breakfast license,
Phemus seemingly turned his blind eye
to the bigotry and violence,
squandering his dole money on coffin nails and stout.
As clouds of his soul slithered from his nostrils,
not a single patron had suspected
that he was a snout, a covert informant
for the *filth*, someone's animated model
given new life to brief; Argonaut in training.

HUNT

The achromatic gloom of the church's stained-glass window
gargled the moon upon it's brittle tongue.
Surrounding homes had extinguished bed-lights,
slipped bookmarks into where stories had faded
and stumbling between the sheltered streetlight,
Claire had returned to the scene of her crime.

Trust nothing. Cats padding behind bins
possessed aerials for whiskers.
Police rustled in the conifers, parroting robins,
and since Acorn Street, she was positively-paranoid
that she was being followed.

The night stilled, deafened by its own hush.
Lifting out the dripping binbag,
Claire ransacked the Sacred Heart's bin
to find what she was after.
The unholiest bouquets of decayed meat
and sour wine dissolved between her digits,
pinned beneath nail, until a scrunched church pamphlet
materialised like a prayer answered.

Francis Ward's funeral was scheduled for Thursday at 10am.
One could always pay their respects in Catholic guilt
and foot the bill upon their deathbed.
Meantime, the hunt was on, for a black dress.

PIXELS

High heavens had become condensed
with extinguished barbeque smoke
caused by the Stevens family's Holy Communion party.
One kid had quit without his waistcoat,
floating like the cherry blossom leaves
ticker-taping down Acorn Street
before half-century old eyes and cancer in the throat
prevented Cheryl from ever lassoing him back.

It was dark now. Late. Curtains closing like eyelids.
Time for shadowy figures to crawl out from bosky estates.
Hid in the corners of forbidden districts
from which one hooded creature
crept past the front window,
            essentially on tip-toe towards the church.
Cheryl had heard tittle-tattle about the murder.
How the church's metal cross had smashed old Frank's head
like an egg: shavings of shell-skull
still visible on the white marble floor.

She followed the figure, closeted by Bridgeton's starless sky
until it came to a halt outside the Sacred Heart.
Holding onioned-breath, Cheryl slowly slipped
a mobile phone out and began recording
the ransacking creature,
zooming in with a thumb and index finger
until a familiar face surfaced from pixels.

She was positive the girl attended Holyrood Secondary
with her eldest son. Farquharson? Perhaps. No.
Wait. F-   erg   Ferguson.

OLD FIRM DAY

               is tense flowers
of blue and green, blossoming inside boozers
where a thick air of language and stale sweat
overflows on to the street.

It is a day to think twice about the colour
of your footwear, nail varnish, contact lens.

In the home, the unwalked dog meditates pavements,
daren't make eye contact if they lose.
The church is well-stocked ciborium's and empty pews.
Is it true priests get free seats at Parkheid?

On trains, no-one wants the day-shift
as the city spins grave colours on the faces of the neutrals.

Trouble is not prejudiced, welcomes all-comers
into its morning-after papers with blades incising faces
and into ribs in the dangerous places
your parents once warned you about.

Southern India, child-labour stitched-flags
stir hatred and poison and for many, this is an enjoyment –
a reason for existing. A sense of belonging.

Keep your head down
if you don't like what you see. Glasgow's about to kick off.

INHERITANCE

It was her solicitor who delivered the news.
Chronic liver disease.
Passed away in her sleep, aged 53.
Phemus brushed the letter, caressing it like a cherished pet,
certifying that it was genuine; no sham letterhead.

Honouring his late father's wishes that upon his mother's death
Phemus would inherit the Military Cross medals
acquired from service in the Falklands
(or whatever riches secured from their sale).

His fingers trembled around a smeared whiskey glass.
His remaining eye, a salty whirlpool
      until it lay on the soldier's letter
passed to his mother on that day in Paddy's Market.
The non-telegram. The ham yarn he had been given.

Already, he knew that the hazy beams of sunlight
lodged inside the throats of clogged Glaswegian chimney lums
would soon hack up robins and sparrows
into its tonic, blue sky
and he would follow wherever they go.

WALK ON

Not the Catholic detectors nor the metal detectors
inside Ibrox stadium had unearthed Danny's intentions.

He could smell himself, swathed
in a lemon-fluorescent jacket standing adjacent
to Deek's red, blue and white inflated face, *s c r e a m i n g*
like it had already happened.

Danny flicked the spring of his mini cleaver pocket knife.
It's cool, stainless steel was light to touch,
creasing lines into his thumbnail. Step forward.

Walk on, walk on, cut a hooooole in his heart, and you'll NE-
veering to one side, Danny was rushed
by two cops on his blind side
sending the weapon spinning
into the loose, rusted grit on the trackside.

Supporters heads spun like plates.
Now, he had become like the roadkill
passed on his way to the stadium; the gape-mouthed,
flame-feathered skull of the fox
screaming back on its mashed torso,
and the savage crack of a solid baton
which would lead to four weeks without any top teeth.

BANKED

The SF61 reg plate indicated that it was game over.
Outside the post office on Main Street,
restraints were wrapped round Joe's wrists
before being propelled into the back seat of the cop car.

In the station at the charge bar,
the turnkey creepily slid on lubricated gloves
used for cavity searches.
It's only love if it's consensual, he jibed
as the officers on either side bent Joe over the cool, steel table.
He was sure one caressed his hair when he did.

Things weren't right. The drugs banked
inside Joe's arsehole were fixed, rigid, coated in waste matter
and just as the turnkey's fingers
clipped on to the paper wrapper,
something *r u p t u r e d*
causing Joe to excrete a sack of muck and brown dust;
a Kinder surprise crumbling all over the jailer's fist.

FOR FUCK SAKE YA FILTHY PIG,
the turnkey shrieked while Joe blew him an air-kiss, retorting
You should have bought me dinner first.

WHOSE FUNERAL?

Funerals of the elderly never appear more heart-breaking
than like the small cluster which had gathered
at Abercromby Street's neglected cemetery
to lay to rest the body of Francis 'Frank' Ward.

DI Jackson leant against the slate-grey stone
watching Frank and Gina's friends with silvery, singed fringes
from lighting cigs on their stoves
throw roses on the coffin,
blowing farewell kisses from arthritic fingertips.

Away, near the vandalised gate pillars,
a young waif of a girl stood on her own,
engraved into the shaded pall of the mourning, morning sky.

Slowly, Jackson bridged the gap over the uncultivated grass
and toppled headstones, setting her hand
on the youngster's shoulder.
Claire? she purred in her ear,
we need to speak away from here.

A crow on a branch acted as ventriloquist's puppet,
screeching from inside Claire without a flinch of her lips
and when the police car slid in first gear
to the rear of where they were standing,
she knew it had been a mistake to come here.

If her boyfriend didn't kill her, then PB would make sure of it.

DEAD MEAT

His tongue vacuumed the truant spaces
where top teeth should be. A disagreeable blue mattress
juxtaposed the navy, sunken eye socket
scanning the yellow, fatty, pockmarked walls
inside the holding cell
where several others had pissed, shit, and choked
on their own vomit. Even finished themselves.

Alarm bells rang inside Danny's ears
when he heard the nasally voice yelling in the cell next door.
Good old Joe. Lifelong pal and partner in crime, Joe.
Joe, in his Amazing Technicolour Dreamcoat
nicked from a rail in Manorgrove
with whom Danny had disclosed
plans to gore a fat, orange fuck.

Et tu, Joe? Danny growled.
Danny? Is that y-

A bucket slammed off the wall. The clang of a death knell
reverberating;
a Reaper's scythe engraving metal.

Danny knew someone had snitched.
The police had rushed him at the first twitch of his blade,
a nanosecond of that first itch, and now the pigs
were goading, prodding him with this *prick* of a friend
in the room next to his.

The stench of dead meat next door
reeked more than the mattress.

GLOAMING

Dissolving his temper into the stonework
of the Tolbooth Steeple at Glasgow Cross,
        Phemus was at a loss for words.

Like Romeo's skulduggery returned, the skyline
was awash in Juliet's blood
and in the lightning-blinks of his irritated eye,
conceptualised heads of witches and prisoners
impaled upon the tower's spikes
howled open-mouthed, barren of tongue.

Phemus's father was not dead, then.
Instead, he had met another.
Fallen for her siren charms then taken her as a lover.

The letter passed to his mother was no army telegram
(expired in 1982), but a warning from Petra Balders
that her boy would come to harm
if he was to ever learn the truth.

Like a black wood breathes in twilight to its ashen bones,
a gloaming inherited his mood,
casting an infernal pall across the Saltmarket belt.

COURT

A cousin loaned him the suit.
The jury would take one look
and expose him for what he was;
a thug ned kitted out in cheap threads.

Do anything but cry. Danny knew that anarchy
was something more than a bottle of hair dye
but something compelled him to change. Shave.
Bleach away the damage. Knot the tie, and then walk
with his newly tennis ball formed head held high.

But he couldn't look his mother in the eye
as he sat isolated inside the accused box.
She had suffered enough
and Danny was slowly becoming a lost cause
to the McAllister family.

Sentenced to six months inside.
Shoe laces and neck size
were becoming two associated companions.
A veneered cupboard's gallows deserve no audience;
a tongue-tied tie-rack to knot top buttons,
rock bottoms.

LOST ARK

The interview room was lemon. Not fresh, but coloured.

Claire heaved, while her estranged mother
analysed the skeletal creature
purporting to be her daughter sat next to her.

Nicotine stains blotched buttons on the tape player.
Claire noticed how yesterday's smoke
seemed to haunt the ceiling light
like the liberated ghosts inside the chest
of the Indiana Jones: *Raiders of the Lost Ark* film.

DI Jackson was firing the questions:
Where have you been staying? Who is your partner?
When did you last visit Edinburgh?
Have you heard of Petra Balders?
Do you know where the Sacred Heart is? Are you a believer
in God? Why were you at the funeral of Francis Ward?

Claire clamped her tongue between teeth
until recorded, grainy footage
depicted Claire rummaging through bins
confirmed fears that she had been followed.
Like the neo-Nazi's in the Indiana film,
Claire's face melted into a puddle of tears,
swallowing hard for the first time.

Drug dealing is a long jail sentence, but murder...
Jackson let the words hang like the gallows.
Waited for the signal to cut the rope.

RENDEZVOUS

The sickly, drained Calton skyline gust ashes on the wind,
spitting crows between its leafless trees.

Phemus adjusted his woollen hat then stepped inside the empty café
where a radio crackled its advert jingle, and Deek's father
lifted his sapped eyes over the newspaper
to casually examine the tall visitor.

He had seen him around. Recognised his lurch,
his twitching frame spotted in the Gallowgate. But not his name.

I believe I may have something
of interest to you, Mr Ronaldson, Phemus inclined.

The two men surveyed one another
then the A4 brown envelope
which had been placed on the counter.
Deek's father slid out photographs
of one Daniel McAllister; would-be executioner of his only son.

And what would you wish for in return?
Deek's father countered.
Phemus's lips coiled, upturned at the corners.

BAIL

Luss was a sliver of Heaven's mirror.
White gold sand melted beneath Claire's bare feet
as seabirds hooted above the frothy, comic opera
which is salty Loch Lomond.

Released on bail, she marvelled at the golden cobwebs
dangling between village hedges.
Treasured the daisy chains children had left
fastened round timber fences
and wheezed at the storm of butterflies
glissading across the azure waters.
This was an alien world. Elysian fields.

A crumpled map given by a Police Officer
informed her that the spectacular mountain
west of her was Ben Lomond
and that small island was Inchmurrin;
the unofficial *Scud Capital* of Scotland.
One day she would visit there. Do yoga.
Wave to the speedboats with her feet.

They would be at Polmadie Bridge by now, handcuff-ready.
Claire rubbed her bruised arm,
breathed in the shady pines then traced the bus times home.

The blue clouds were moving in.

PREACHER

Sixty-six days, shrilled the lad next to Danny,
spitting flakes of salt fish and porridge
across the table and over the listening party.

Danny's mind meandered.

If Bobby Sands' legacy was his hunger-strike,
then this one would be remembered
for his unbridled nostril hair and impotence in self-grooming
        yet something about this stranger appealed.

His thick, Limerick-accent preached like a true believer
that British imperialism
had raped, stolen from, and defiled Ireland.

One of the other prisoners sneered,
snorted derision at the wild man
conducting his daily breakfast rant.

Without warning, the preacher manifested the cactus plant
usually reserved for his windowsill
and propelled it squarely and firmly
into the face of the mocking creature.
All future breakfasts
would now be about guerrilla warfare and honour.

SETBACKS

Structurally unsafe, local councillors had agreed
that Polmadie Bridge was to be demolished
leaving them with no fixed abode.

Claire had also vanished. He had cautioned her
to always keep her dirty phone charged
but each call redirected to answerphone.

Then there was PB's boys.
Being in four-figured debt to six-foot plus slabs of meat,
he had opted to use the goods
then pollute the surplus with adulterants
such as waterproof shoe polish and laundry detergent.
And don't forget Danny. Spitting his dummy,
threatening to carve him open and grind his body
for the local pig farms to enjoy.
He knew he was capable of carrying out such threats.

Hands masked his grizzled, boyish face –
a modern-day martyr of the paper round
when police sprung out from the long grass,
shoving his nose into the repugnant ground
and cuffing his hands behind his back.

Joseph Colvan, I am arresting you on suspicion
of the murder of Francis Ward,
and as one eye rolled towards DI Jackson,
she swore she could hear a snort
and a whimpered sigh of relief escape from the suspect.

SHIPMENT

Loose lips sink shipments. House whisky cackling aside,
the two old, flat capped boys inside the Tolbooth Bar
had lowered their voices to hide their schemes.

Semi-automatic ArmaLite AR-15's and detachable magazines
were easy to break into parts.
These had proven popular with Provo farmers
overpowered by British troops during the early scraps
of what became known as The Troubles.

The weapons would be smuggled in crates
laden with white sports socks.
A pickup point had been arranged
at Cairnryan Port, wherein a messenger would transport the box
up the A77 to an agreed drop-off spot
on the outskirts of Glasgow.

The job was worth two thousand notes
and word was that there was a boy just released
from a short-term prison stint identified to carry out the errand.
Below the television in the corner of the pub,
Phemus was using his military-acquired skills
to lip-read, squinting his remaining eye
to take heed of every detail.

The police would pay him well for such information
but now new priorities were leading his reasoning.

PATHWAY

Rain pummelled on the classroom window,
muddling watercolours of raincoated staff huddled outside,
puffing on their interval fags.
Claire's prison pathway out of drugs
was now three months passed
and the self-harming reduced to extracting eyelashes.
A vast improvement on her recent past.

EMAP had initially reconnected
her to her mother. Now, visits. Gifts.
A kiss on each occasion after several heart-to-hearts.

Claire's father was a *Wanted*, unwanted man.
Vanished, without a trace,
DI Jackson had promised her justice.
That one day, she would see his face
crestfallen. Imprisoned. Guilty of rape.
For now, all she could do was wait.

Another month of clean saliva samples
and with good behaviour, she could be released soon.
It had been so long since she last felt this human.

Claire choked up and was excused to the bathroom
(supervised) then cried a rainstorm,
tinting the wash hand basin with tapered, cosmetic rainbows.

*EMAP – *Email A Prisoner*

CRUCIFIXION

DI Atkinson's phone spasmed in the dark
like lightning in a cheap horror film.

It was Dumfries & Galloway Special Branch.
A young man had been apprehended.
Found forsaken in a deserted car park close to The Merchant's House
where he had been crucified to the driver's seat
inside a white transit van by two men possessing a nail-gun.

Atkinson joined the floating, squiggly dots
dancing in the dark of his bedroom.

This tactic had once been employed by Glaswegian assassins.
Fanatics of barbarous, hard-hearted executions
but what was its significance to his investigation?
The soft, Southern Scotland voice explained
that the crucified party was Si Galbraith
and that the van was intended to convey weapons
on behalf of the IRA. Worse still, Mr Galbraith's friend was missing
and McAllister was his name.

RECCE

Military grade night vision gear mutated him into a Kafka story;
pickle-leaved pelt, bugged optics.

A high-walled defence and plugged brew of birds' nests
in the garden's dense trees would deter most men
but through a ghost's balaclava of persistent mist,
the snowy octopus tentacles
of Petra Balders' hair
reflected in the kitchen's silver toaster;
an Irish banshee wailing someone's mortality.

By the third recce, car registrations were imprinted in the mind.
The times her sons visited.
The nights she was alone.

PEAK

A glass-firework burst against the kitchen wall.

Petra Balders had instantaneously transformed
into a hideous gorgon. Albino snakes
hissed upon her contorted, green skull,
pretzeled by the news her sons had just divulged.

Nobody fucking steals from me.

The colossal beasts crouched before the termagant,
their mis-shaped heads bowed to deflect the brunt
of any further articles hurled at them.

I'm going to find the boy in the hospital.
In the meantime, find those accountable –
then give them the fairy rock.

BARGAINING

In hospital twilight, Petra Balders inched through the fire exit,
locating Si's private bedroom in a matter of minutes.

Sleep interrupted, his eyes intensified
on sight of Petra's grave face looming over his;
one withered hand clamped over his box-taped mouth.

Do you know what 'degloving' means, young man?
The old lady hoisted his gown, pursing her sour mouth
and licking her lips upon the first sight
of his inopportune, upright dick.

Squeezing one of the mutilated hands,
Balders yanked the mouth-tape,
purring bitter wine-grapes into his ear, bargaining genitals
in return for names, details, or spotted cars
of those responsible for the theft of her AR's.

Stammering, Si spluttered *Si – Si – Cy – cyclops*
then Petra clamped her incisors down on his bollocks.

CURLING

Blood seeped out the seat of his trousers
on to the ice like syrup over a slushie.
Rotary, power tools had been used
until consciousness pervaded but now,
restrained at the wrists and ankles in Saltire-reverse position,
the victim detected more suffering was to follow.

Blearily, he could see the outlines of a Reapers trinity, hooded
in an ogre's huddle, while a fourth – the tallest of all –
flashed an imperilling smile.
It was he who held the heavy stone in his hand.

Swinging his arm back from Heaven to Hell,
Greeber's colossal strength hurled
the skating gravestone towards him
until the skull burst like an eggshell
and bled crimson thought-bubbles over the rink.

SECURITY

Even before the finger of security light
flared to the rear of her home, PB knew she was not alone.

Her boys were out, *sweeping* Shane Ferguson
into his next life and someone had known
Chateau Balders was prime to strike.
Behind the black marble breakfast bar
and it's dangling, overheard champagne glasses,
she silently cocked the semi-auto revolver.
Her assassin-in-waiting was dirty bath water
inside her strong, surging, cleansing river.

Then, *a BLAST* spun the kitchen
into a blackened, smoking midden,
making ear-rings from glass
and piercings of tongue, cheek and hands.

She was alive, just, spluttering dust, scorched.
Through the dense smoke at the back door,
a ghost with a hole where one eye should be
levitated towards her,
effortlessly lifting her upon its broad shoulder
and carried her into a syncope.

STRAW MAN

This was the countryside where giant, metallic birds
with 200ft blade spans silently rolled in the winds
and where a parachutist on his first solo jump
was once diced into chunks of dog food by a volatile gust.
DI Atkinson had been the first on the scene
of that disgusting day.

In the centre of a family-visited pumpkin patch
sited on the outskirts of Glasgow, a neglected scarecrow
was fastened to a wooden cross frame
using three-inch nails and baling twine to hold it upright.

Its aberrant assemble comprised of gardening glove hands,
a cherry-black chequered shirt,
squalid jeans with encrusted dirt and a pillowcase-hooded face
where a leather belt girdled straw from spilling out its base.

Constable Costello steadily aimed his torch
as DI Atkinson raised the cloth
before tumbling backwards into sod and grunge.

Underneath it had teeth inside its rotten, gaping mouth
and an acrid, oat-coloured tongue
to haunt any crow's crippled dreams.
The victim had been suffocated
and wilfully, in the lucid moonbeams,
situated somewhere he'd be found before Hallowe'en.

The Forensics squad would arrive in less than fifteen minutes
but Atkinson already knew that his victim
was Danny McAllister from the Calton.

TABLOID HAIKU

TOLBOOTH REGULAR
SLAIN AT CLOSED ICE RINK CENTRE.
REPUBLICAN LINKS.

ANALYSIS

Forensics had quickly distinguished
the blue hone granite of an Ailsa Craig curling stone
had been used to finish both Shane Ferguson and Danny off.
Sapphire, cross-stitching
situated where the lid of the skull should be,
remoulding Danny into some sort of Frankenstein's Monster,
green and decaying on a makeshift table.

Atkinson blew cigarette smoke
against a fairy storm of dandelion heads
bobbing across the pumpkin patch.
If the Balders family were to blame,
they wouldn't be easy to catch
but there couldn't be many manufacturers
who produced such a unique stone.

Thumbing an Airwave remote control through fingerless gloves,
he called the office and instructed the SIO to direct her analysts
to investigate any Ailsa Craig stone purchases
over the last twenty-four months.
Returned into white paper suit,
Atkinson took one final look
at the melding straw and brain pulp,
as stomach-churning as the unpalatable wheat and berry cereal
he had gulped down this morning
and exiting the forensic tent,
prepared himself to visit the McAllister family home.

SHREDDED

Like father, like daughter.
Shane Ferguson had been working for the Balders.

Not in the drugs market but trafficking firearms, ammunition,
procurement of weapons for Republican dissidents
via ferry crossings – and failed for the last time.

DI Lisa Jackson let the tea cool in her cupped hands
while Claire and her mum frustratingly took turns
to ask the obvious questions.
Jackson was as angry as both women
that no apology or explanation would be forthcoming
but time was of the essence.
Two murders in twenty-four hours,
both using Ailsa Craig produced stones.

Jackson left the women alone with their thoughts;
as shredded as their nerves and family albums.

GRAVE

Silvery clouds parted
like a thousand-piece jigsaw
patterned with the face of God.
Clippings of His wispy beard
floated, revealing dark, bruised eyes of star-crossed haters
Petra recognised only too well.

The moon was a big toe, a sheared nail –
or was it her own? Too pale to belong to a human.
Spades of soil blunted her sight,
wad nostrils thick like chocolate cake
until her shallow grave failed to resonate with the sound
of her own muffled scream.

Perhaps someday, a school forestry excursion group
would investigate these woods.
Scrutinise the indented terrain.
Break up the earth then yell for their half-witted teacher
to look at the animal bones they have discovered.

WHALE TAPES

A series of clicks, whistles and whale groans
thronged in the small hallway of the McAllister's home.

A holy font was bolted to a wall outside the living-room
where a cosmic-sized Sacred Heart
was squarely-lit with dressing room bulbs
and a crude, painted depiction of Tommy Burns
perched alongside.

Mrs McAllister already knew Danny was dead.
She either had a sixth sense or was spiritually-inbred
judging by her cross-eyed, sedated state.

Even the weary sigh from Mr McAllister
revealed a thick, Irish accent
when the distressing news was delivered.
A cigarette was all he could use to make sense.

After all questions had been posed,
DI Atkinson passed his condolences on a card
with his number (should anything spring to mind)
and as he closed the front door behind him,
he swore he could distinctly hear
the Hail Mary prayer being read aloud

                by Free Willy.

SAFE HOUSE

Off the beaten track, the covert cop
hoisted the holdall out the car-boot
and led Phemus through the heavy oak door
of the sea-whipped fisherman's cottage
where his new life would begin.
Ancient grazing rights permitted sheep
to rove outside, mix with cyclist tourists
and local dialects; animated postcards
bestowed with lungs and skin and flatulence.

He had seen such intense seascapes in paintings
hung over pub fireplaces where stuffed fox carcasses
and redcoat hunts were conventional stock
but the unsmoked sea spray lashing
the unsullied, tendered gardens
were as foreign and distant as the medieval re-enactments
celebrated in the "things to do" pamphlet.

Drawing the last drag from a cigarette,
the cop honked like the nearby seals
when he revealed to Phemus
that his new career would be as a florist
before returning to his rust bucket and spluttering southwards
towards the sweet pollution of a city
Phemus would never breathe in again.

CLUBBING

She had needed to leave the house. A night out.
Rain threatened to uncoil
Claire's straightened, chestnut-dyed hair
but inside the shaded, fog-lights of the throbbing nightclub,
the narcotically-charged hedonism of a dancefloor
was an idyllic Arcadia, a sought chimera
she had been unable to get near for most of her still-young life.

Chambers rumbled music into the floorboards,
manipulating frequencies and voice messages
from her deceased father in Hell below her.
Claire sizzled, dancing on a grave, waving to the neon spirits
discharging from the living's breath.

Long-lost school friends embraced her, soaking in the elements,
the sweat of one another's safe haven arms.
How beautiful the world could look when a moon-sized pill
dissolved all ills and problems.

Toffee-hearted, Claire melted into the music
and
drifted
out
the
exit.

LIGHTNING STRIKES

It never rains but it pours. A fire raged at Petra Balders' home.
Prime suspect for recent murders but now, she was as alone
as the unmarked graves of several of her victims.
DI Atkinson groaned like bagpipes.

The house had been extinguished and now,
inside, the sooty jawbone of a funeral furnace
vented like one of PC Costello's vape kits.

Atkinson punted one of the apples lying on the scorched ground
directly into the carved mouth of a nearby Jack-o'-lantern.
It's creepy, chiselled crevice
reminded the DI of yesterday's pumpkin patch
where Danny McAllister's pulped corpse
had been discovered. Hallowe'en
was no religious holiday to celebrate.

Yet if Balders was McAllister's murder suspect
but had vanished simultaneously,
then wasn't there the possibility
that someone else was responsible and had possibly
disposed of her in the same territory?
The hunch slammed his head like a spade.
Catching his wind, Atkinson's voice became a bugle
in the rain, pitching *All units...*'

CHIPS PROTOCOL

The city had a queer air about it.
Buchanan Street's ramshackle piper
repeatedly discharged 'Flowers Of The Forest'
as Deek greedily demolished
the extra chips in his sausage supper.
His fat belly rumbled like the nightclub basslines
where entrance signs plastered his swollen face in pink hues.

Merchant City girls clad in shimmering Diana Ross silver coats
pulled over their bleached-blonde heads
to protect them from the downpour giggled and galloped
between flashing, sparky bars
like shooting stars gliding in the dark.

Spare one, big lad?
Deek spun round. A pretty, petite brunette
pointed one xylophonic fingernail
to his near-empty carton
and like a Film Director shouting 'Action'
a firework illuminated the sky on cue
and kindled a bonfire inside of him.

REQUIEM

Black sails fluttered. Pirate flags
hired for the stormy Glasgow skyline.

A circus of crows flapped absurdly,
cawing in time with the thunder
and DI Atkinson's firm instructions.
The tracker dogs, gnashing at his bluster, barked blue murder
as several torches zigzagged
every corner of the pumpkin patch,
knowing time was of the essence.

This was no Requiem mass.
It was close to where Danny had been discovered.
Soil was freshly turned, burnt side up, bubbling in rainwater.
Sodden officers in anoraks, dragged out from behind desks,
speed-typed spades, slinging earth flying in all directions.

No coffin. One officer struck bone, hand,
black as the Burntisland sand he had grown up with.
Spades were laid to the side as all began frantically
raking, scraping, scrabbling at the clay
until the Hallowe'en horror mask
of one Petra Balders materialised.

A pulse, as faint
as memories of Atkinson's Canary Islands holiday;
apparent as the remnants of his tan.

MOLLY

Her flat could have doubled as one of Deek's shoeboxes.
Half a life lay on her bed – clothes
which smelled of everything she cooked,
scattered books, a pair of snakeskin shoes.
Long, false lashes upturned
like small tarantulas had shed their exoskeletons.

The practical challenges of removing clothes
vexed Deek. Passing, ground-floor buses
cast unfavourable spotlights on his ample, meaty posterior
through the caved-in blinds, wilting at the sight.
She didn't seem to mind.

The miniature fridge hummed its love-songs
as Deek kissed her nape, grazing
the tattoo of a cartoon bat upon her tiny shoulder.
Strangers who walked past cast quick glances
in the window, giggling, maybe filming
but never stopping for long
before he realised that something was wrong.

The tennis-returned grunts had stopped
and the chaos of the room shrunk, becoming dumb, mute.
He lifted his head. Shook the girl until her head lolled.
Eyes like full moons, blood running from her nose
like a rose sprouting from a nostril.

It would be a full four minutes
before Deek located his mobile
to summon the hospital
and an eternity before an ambulance appeared.

MODUS OPERANDI

The beermat had been picked clean.
A clattering bell rung for last orders,
awakening DI Atkinson from his daydream
inside the near-empty State Bar when   it   clicked.
Rather, it bonged. Clanged. A bombshell of clarity sang
like one of those angelic *HA-LLE-LU-JAH* moments
directors of films loved to use to express a point.

A book propped behind the bar
brooded the 1960s hallmark crucifixions
of one Peter Ronaldson but since his death
such modus operandi had been all but forgotten.

Pitt Street's abandoned HQ phantoms
mirrored the obese moon's beam
as Atkinson bounded into a lit taxi,
spitting a destination and the name *Ronaldson*
into an unsuspecting driver's ear
and the index held by the National Records of Scotland.

STANDOFF

He wouldn't be taken. Not like his brothers.
Greeber thrashed the small sword in the kitchen,
carving the gap between him and the officers
with a stuttering hand.

We just want to talk, cooed one burly hombre.
A stab-proof vest clung to the cop's body
like a TV set wad up his jouk.

They had reached stalemate when the taser was administered
before Greeber could object,
zapping his bones with barbed electrodes.

The sword clanged on the tiled floor
just before Greeber's skull followed suit
and leather-buckled boots rained down.

FLORIST

His face crinkles, a crumpled toffee paper
licked clean, squinting at invisible stones in shoes
which thorn his calloused soles.
The customer detects raven feathers
beating under his rolled sleeves. Tattooed initials of names
upon the wing-tips; birds now buried in flowerpots.

Her child dissolves into the small digital window
which is his world, lit by the crude bare bulbs
framing a lapsed Swimming World poster on the glass.
Behind the till, Phemus's faint scars smile, masking
all that he's seen, knows, and outlasted.
A prosthetic hand, gloved as a secret.

He sees it; trained to. Wishes it gone; the pity
of strangers. She studies him for too long,
the wreath of a captor's regard, but then softens
like December's daylight. Her late husband
cradle songs inside a silver locket, rendering
her to move on with the remainder of her young life.

He knows flowers well, slept in fields
where war never belonged
and jewels sprouted out of turbid tread.
From the ashes of this year's St Valentine's stock,
he pulls the pin from a buttercup
and pitches his grenade heart;
blinded by the impact.

TOXICOLOGY

Her eyes felt like solid gravestones
with her name engraved on the backs of the lids.
A drip attached itself to her arm threaded by a red tube
running with the gift of life
from someone undoubtedly better than her.

Claire's mother was folded in a chair like crumpled decoupage;
a 'Get Well Soon' card in human form
while outside the window, morbid crows
blinked their yellow beady eyes, multiplying in a Reaper's fog.

In the bed next to her, the blue girl was disconnected by nurses
while doctors scribbling in clipboards
pursed talented, foreign lips at the questions
which intruding Police Officers were asking.

Just before the white curtain was drawn,
Claire swore she could see the fog gravitate
towards the blue girl,
cupping vapoury fingers to catch her transit soul
when it coasts out from her gaping mouth.

BLOODSUCKING

A half-century of serenity sat before DI Atkinson.
Jim Ronaldson sat cross-armed, captivated
by the two-way mirror
which was currently scrutinising his body language,
peculiar ticks, the slightest hint of a fart when quizzed
about Danny McAllister's death
and the shallow grave in which
Petra Balders had been discovered in.

No comment, ricocheted off the walls so often
that even the tape machine had begun
to sound like it was yawning. Atkinson wasn't done yet.

Derek was the target of an attack by McAllister, was he not?
No comment.
Someone has to make a lesson out of these wee Fenian
                                        scumbags, eh?
                                        No comment.
Our intelligence provides that there were two men there that
                                      night at Cairnryan.
                                        No comment.
Your business has become the subject of a money laundering
                                        investigation.
                                        No comment.
Ronaldson was sweating. Arm-pits never lie
and Atkinson knew the time was right to strike.

*I should inform you that earlier this morning, Derek was found
in the company of a young lady who had overdosed
on ecstasy we believe to be MDMA.
I must advise you that the young lady
has since passed away and your son is currently being detained
for the supply of this substance.*

Ronaldson winced. Balls tightly secure in vice.

Jim. Who was the other man with you in Cairnryan
on the night in question?

Ronaldson knew that he was out of options.
Confess, or else Deek would be held accountable
before trial. Jailed without rationale.

The accused squirmed, shifting into a new position.
The mirror leant its glass ears in
as Ronaldson weakly announced the name
which would turn Atkinson's face into the carved Jack-o'-lantern
he had seen in Petra Balders garden.

GIRVAN

The dangling pendant moon
reflected in the water at Girvan harbour
like the corner of a Ouija board
moved by the fingers of stars.
Tommy Greeber, Snr loved it here.

Lost in the gothic bride veil of a cobweb,
trails of his exhaled smoke appeared to clump together.
A white mass forming until the apparent exhaust fumes
transformed his face into
a skull from the Sicilian catacombs –

'POLICE' on the bonnet of whatever he just breathed out.

What now?

OMNIPRESENT

He had been there all along. Seamus Walsh.
At the Tolbooth, when Shane Ferguson
had talked weapons, shipments and moorings.
At Girvan, when Greeber Snr implicated his own son
by trading off scraps of Ailsa Craig stone.
When the Balders boys were at the ice rink,
he had been waiting outside Petra Balders' home.

At Cairnryan, when Danny McAllister was kidnapped
and then he assisted Jim Ronaldson
in Simon Galbraith's crucifixion.
Then at the pumpkin patch, plotting and manipulating
Danny's execution.

And now, he had a new home, living alone in the north
and working in a flower store,
all at the expense of Police Scotland.

DI Atkinson grimaced, stubbing his cigarette
into the permanently-clean paving stones
outside the Scottish Crime Campus
then led the team briefing
as to how exactly they were going to do this.

CONVOY

Usually the ice-blue glacial glens leading to the north of Scotland
crystallised the eyes of the stags and deer –
the purest, alien creatures which Atkinson ever beheld.

However, as the convoy proceeded
deeper into the Highland's gloaming,
a pall of the otherworld's night washerwomen
sousing clothing in the range brooks
prompted vigorous rubbing of the DI's heavy eyes.
Rain clouds were forming.

DS Costello's snoring
coalesced with the disappearing radio signal.
Twinkles of bat eyes, puffins, something on the slopes
seemed to follow them, then evanesce
with the turning of each road bend.

Atkinson's stomach sank hard
like the student found in the Clyde
with rocks in his backpack;
hands tied together with festival wristbands.
An informant gone bad meant his head was on a plate.
The taste of a bad apple, rotting in his mouth.

ZOOM

He has always loved the power of zooming.
Thumb and forefinger parting on mobile phone,
he can magnify, amplify, intensify the veins of flower petals,
the coruscating disco of stars, the cerise hem of robin feathers.
The only toy he had ever owned was a vandalised telescope
he discovered in the children's home.
Phemus had strayed into galaxies,
other children's families and agonised
over the famine of his own ancestry until sleep stalled the sting.
Now, surveillance soothes the soul. Pixels propagate his choice
to leave with her, the flower shop girl and child,
and begin their new lives in the wild blossom of Scandinavia.

His covert camera on a nearby telegraph pole
follows the masked, camouflaged figures
darting round the snowy borders of the vacated fisherman's cottage.
Windows shatter. A heavy beam splinters the door.

He zooms, boosting the repulsed features of DI Atkinson, bewildered.
Bound now to have discovered the blue stone
of the home-made knuckledusters on the kitchen table.

NAMES

i.

Names could be queer things.
Had he not been called something else before?
His mind reclined like a psychiatrist's couch.
A black, leathery mooring for his thoughts:

Equipped with lettuce, jam jars.
His father's large, calloused hand
holding his own dirtied, tiny paw
as they scooped tadpoles from the bomb ponds.
The sky scorching an irregular orange.

Then returning home, the Irish cadence
of his mother's scorn for *removing the boi from scoil*
when education was paramount.

It wasn't Walsh, then. Not quite so singular.
Something longer. Harsher. Like   Greeber.

ii.

Haiku

Three boys raised Balders.
Youngest raised as a Greeber
post-split with mother.

Eldest son estranged.
Mother may have changed name to
Walsh. First name, Seamus.

END CREDITS

If this was Eastenders, drums would be rolling
    doof-doof...doof-doof-doof
but unfortunately for Tommy Greeber Snr,
his deadpan expression was being captured by no cameras.
Only proof of shaved Ailsa Craig stone inside a plastic pouch
was all the drama that Girvan Police Station
would be enjoying tonight.

DI Atkinson's stony air and lifeless stare foretell what lay ahead
and like the bottle of the DI's mineral water,
his patience was positively lukewarm.
Greeber Snr fidgeted, fumbling
with one of the many sovereign rings
on his large, Bratwurst fingers.
He was nothing more than a pawn. A con.
A wrong 'un, controlled by Petra Balders
after their relationship had soured and became, just, business.

Now, a photograph of his eldest was presented.
Not that the boat owner recognised the image as Seamus.
Yes. This was the man who had visited
and paid a large sum for so little in return.

Atkinson's waxed eyebrow arched
and as he divulged the identity to the accused,
Greeber Snr's ear drums bludgeoned a familiar theme tune.

SENTENCE

Tossed teabags tarnished the corroding kitchen sink
where clattering crockery cumulated,
straining the plastic dish rack

and the musty stink of the unemptied cat litter box
violated the hallway where the family pictures grimaced
while mother whined like bagpipes or a dolorous violinist.

Deek's father was sentenced to *Life* for the grimmest cruelties
his son had never truly known
such as the disposal of one enemy's baby
down a bin chute in the high flats
after a dispute between families provoked merciless attacks
which the police could never prove.

Perhaps Jim Ronaldson's Masonry brothers
could grouse the verdict – acquit some of the indictment,
alleviate the punishment
but as Deek watched the 6 o' clock news,
straining to listen between his mother's convulsive gasps,
in his heart he knew he had seen the last
of his father as he had perceived him.

MIRACLES

Like sunflowers, she liked to hum.
Miracles appeared all around them.
In the ballads of rockslides when elves scampered, hiding
beneath hillside stones on the Faroes agrestic heathlands.

In a temporary dwam, she marvelled at the bees
dancing maps and the light-eating plants
they flitted between.

Now the twinned faces of Janus
contemplating both future and past seemed to surface
in the champagne-sprayed waves
spuming upon the harbour

where her lover, Seamus, prayed to the Roman God
for keys to gates, doorways;
a temple in which she could believe in.

FAIRY-TALE

Phemus grinned broadly into the commotion.
Puffins jumbled around
like claw cranes frustratingly hoist then relinquish
soft toys behind acrylic sheets of glass
while liquid fireworks stormed out from whales' blowholes
into the eternal gloom of the Faroes makeshift Twilight Zone.

Ragtime locals shimmied
like flapjack octopus on ocean floors,
carrying weighty, werewolf furs
upon their heads and shoulders,
protected from waves cannoning off the black cliffs
spitting four-pointed starfish
into the abyss of pelican bills.

Not since his Bootneck days
had he felt *so*   alive, feverish.

Fairy-tales from fairy rocks were to be believed in.

She dissolves into his giant frame
cooing at the faces in the waves,
the surf's stampeding horses,
toxic eels bending into the letters of her name
and one final kiss later,
launches her silver locket
into the midnight thunderclap.

Acknowledgments

Thank you to both Sheila Wakefield, Founding Editor at Red Squirrel Press and the Scottish Writers' Centre for providing me with the opportunity to write the first ever crime novel entirely in verse.

I would also like to extend my gratitude to those who have opened doors for crime poetry to be given a platform, namely the Director of Bloody Scotland – Bob McDevitt, David Linklater, Sandra Ireland, and all the organisers at the Noir At The Bar events in Scotland who tirelessly support crime writers with their time and energy.

Further thanks to William McIntyre for legal advice and Gerry Cambridge for typesetting and design.

A NOTE ON THE TYPE

This book is set in Swift Neue LT Pro, type designer Gerard Unger's expanded 2009 re-issue of his 1985 classic, Swift. Neue Swift adds numerous weights to its precursor and is a versatile typeface suitable for a range of uses, including poetry.